A Moment with God

For:

From:

A Moment with God for Mothers

PRAYERS FOR EVERY MOTHER

Margaret Anne Huffman

Abingdon Press
Nashville

A Moment with God for Mothers

PRAYERS FOR EVERY MOTHER

This book is printed on acid-free paper.

ISBN 978-1-4267-4589-8

Scripture quotations unless noted otherwise are from the Common English Bible. Copyright © 2011 by the Common English Bible. All rights reserved. Used by permission. www.CommonEnglishBible.com.

Those noted NRSV are from the New Revised Standard Version of the Bible, copyright 1989, Division of Christian Education of the National Council of the Churches of Christ in the United States of America. Used by permission. All rights reserved.

Verses marked (TLB) are taken from *The Living Bible* © 1971. Used by permission of Tyndale House Publishers, Inc., Wheaton, IL 60189. All rights reserved.

11 12 13 14 15 16 17 18 19 20—10 9 8 7 6 5 4 3 2 1
MANUFACTURED IN MEXICO

CONTENTS

Becoming a Mother

You are the one who created
my innermost parts; you knit me together
while I was still in my mother's womb.
I give thanks to you
that I was marvelously set apart.

—PSALM 139:13-14

COME DANCE WITH ME, O God, in this cumbersome, oversized waltz of new life.

I love my amazing body! It blooms and hovers over the tiny being cradled near my heart, as if already on my lap. My cravings are rehearsals for a lifetime of yearnings on behalf of this child.

Be with this child. Be with me, too; for in this conception and gestation, I'm also growing a new me, a mother—a blessed creation.

Lost Sleep

*I will lie down and fall asleep in peace
because you alone, LORD,
let me live in safety.*

—PSALM 4:8

THE HIDDEN "EXTRAS" of mothering overwhelm me: the need to be constantly vigilant, wily, wise, awake—especially awake, O God of midnight feedings.

Reality is revising my fantasy, just as the first dirty diapers transformed my cute nursery into a real baby's home.

Even as I reel from reality, I feel you in my family, in friends, in breasts that tingle at a baby's cry, in ears that hear the cry before it is fully made.

I'm not alone—words for a lullaby. And, dear God, may it bring sleep through the night.

Home, Dusty Home

A false balance is an abomination

—PROVERBS 11:1 NRSV

CAN DUST BE BEAUTIFUL and clutter charming? I hope so, for I'm providing a live-as-it-really-is sort of home. Otherwise, I see only muddy footprints, not the child who made them. Forgive me when I say, "Wipe your feet" before I say, "Hello."

You're in our lives to build relationships, not to monitor our closets. I feel your blessing on my dog-eared home—in sunbeams shining on scattered toys; in rainbows of spilled crayons; in dust motes dancing, like children singing "Ring Around the Rosie."

When I get too persnickety and alarmingly tidy, shake me up like a snow globe, so I can be real—truly, messily, and welcomingly real.

Helping Little Ones Cope

The LORD will guide you continually.
—ISAIAH 58:11

"READ IT AGAIN." "Let's play it again." "Do it again, Mommy."

O, Lord, I'm dizzy from kids wanting to repeat everything. I've spent hours playing "dentist"—tomorrow is the first visit.

Bless my little ones' over-and-over style of coping—coping with shots, "firsts," moving day, new siblings. They rehearse and repeat in play so the scary parts are manageable—so they can learn their lines.

Hold the script while I rehearse my lines: "You can do this." I'm honored to have a recurring role in their rehearsals, encores, and reruns: Mom, a seasoned stand-in.

Discouraged

*"If you have faith the size of a mustard seed . . .
there will be nothing that you can't do."*

—Matthew 17:20

MY EFFORTS are disappearing like sand down a rabbit hole. I peer after it as the kids ignore me—again.

Before I get too discouraged, remind me, God, of mustard seeds, to notice the small things they do which suggest that my messages are getting through.

Today I noticed _____.

Help me cast motherly bread on the waters and trust your process. Kids are not a "done deal," no matter what today is like. From sand seemingly shoved down a hole can come seashores, sand castles, and majestic dunes. Keep me out of the builders' way while they decide what to do with my grains of truth.

Following Mary's Example

Let love guide your life.

—Colossians 3:14 TLB

WHOSE ROAD MAP of mothering shall I follow? Inspire me, wise and loving God, to be like your daughter Mary, who:

- went on a hunch and an angel's say-so.
- trusted her intuition to follow you, turning a deaf ear to critics as she acknowledged deeper truths.
- pondered in her heart and didn't talk too much.
- offered a warm hearth to kith and kin.

Point me beyond the portrait of Mary—daubed sweetly in blue gown and golden-haloed smile—to the mama Mary, who patched her son's robe, made his favorite foods, and went about her life while supporting his from the edges. Give me wisdom to go and do likewise.

Hurting for My Child

You grew weary in your search,
but you never gave up. You strengthened
yourself and went on.

—Isaiah 57:10 TLB

LIKE A TODDLER who falls more than she stands, I'm pulling myself upright in the aftermath of hurt to my child. You are the first to weep; calamity is never your will.

I know you as companion, God of mending hearts. I praise you for the gift of maternal resilience. I think of Mary and other mothers who have hurt and gone on. In their names, turn my grief into action, my rage into redemptive inspiration. Unleash my maternal creativity to help lighten a dark world.

In the Company of Mothers

Two are better than one, because… if they fall,
one will lift up the other…. A threefold cord
is not quickly broken.

—ECCLESIASTES 4:9-12 NRSV

I HEARD THEM before I saw them.

Migrating geese stopped overnight on my river, calling one another onto shore. At dawn, calling again, they lifted off. O Lord, I envy their flock, for mothering feels solitary.

Reassure me, God of nests and flight, that just as geese don't travel alone, neither do you intend for me to mother alone. Thank you for the resources of my foremothers, of mentoring friends who've weathered all the childhood stages, of the seasons of life. Guide me to use them as food for the journey.

Blessings for My Child

"Allow the children to come to me."

—MARK 10:14

O GOD, bless my child, who is...

... milk mustaches, snaggle-tooth grins;
Let the little children come.

... tree climber, sand-pile architect, chef, and
inventor;
Forbid none of them, even

... neon-haired teen with pierced body parts;
this child, too, a beloved renegade;

... student, both cocky and shy, foolish and wise,
seeking My will by daring to dream;

... grown-up visionary and doer,
using My gifts to build a new world.

*This is OUR child, a blessing to us both, for to such
belongs My kingdom.*

25

Hurry Up!

It's wonderful to be young!
Enjoy every minute of it!
—ECCLESIASTES 11:9 TLB

HOW MANY TIMES a day do I say, "Hurry, kids"? Too many, no matter the tally. Babies are scheduled like mini-executives, putting away childish things before the new has worn off.

Intervene, O God, lest my kids never know the joy of dawdling, puttering, "wasting time" on swings, stumps, and garden gates.

Forgive me for being a thief in the night, snatching away their childhood.

Send me to sit beneath your sky with the kids, to learn star names, to find cloud faces, to "be still, and know…" (Psalm 46:10 NRSV). Stars and wind can't be rushed; neither can childhood.

Interruptions

Children are a gift from God.
—PSALM 127:3 TLB

I'M JUST RETURNING from a treehouse picnic—delicious food, great conversation. And to think, dear God, I almost didn't go.

Give me energy when I cannot handle one more interruption, then here comes a child who needs a hug, or a companion on sofa-cushion boats, or a teen with music to play or a movie to debate.

Keep me approachable and ready to venture into the world of my children. Help me do it now, while they're young and our relationship is full of wonder.

Then when pretend becomes reality—sometimes harsh and painful—I'll still be invited to share, to listen.

Simple Wonders

God ... richly provides everything
for our enjoyment.

—1 TIMOTHY 6:17

KIDS MAY HAVE interactive computers, but I, O God, can share a lifetime of simple pleasures a gazillion times more awesome. I know how to make invisible ink and watermelon-rind teeth, how to call birds and name stars.

Help me kindle kids' delight in everyday wonders. Eyes used to computer/TV screens are prone to look right past 'coon pawprints in the mud, a falling star, a robin's nest. It's up to me to lure their gazes away from gadgets and self.

Guide our pilgrimage to childhood. The kids and I are making a U-turn and heading there, awestruck and delighted by the simple wonders of your hand.

Finding Time for Prayer

Pray continually.
—1 THESSALONIANS 5:17

LIKE A SOCK lost in the dryer, I've misplaced my prayers. In between laundry, carpooling, working, picking up toys, and slapping together sandwiches, I pray at you, not to you—tossing off a prayer, a plea, a thank you. Sometimes, God of all the time in the world, mealtime grace is as good as it gets.

Help me see the connection between our relationship and the ones I have with others, especially the children. I use them as excuses for not praying, although they're a prime reason to pray.

Make me clever enough to find pockets of time when we can meet. Help me be still and know who you are and who you know me to be: a beloved daughter who can find time.

Teaching Discernment

Wisdom is found on the lips
of those who have understanding.

—Proverbs 10:13

PART ANGEL, PART IMP—kids at the grocery store are also part con artist. How, wise God, can I say no to a new cereal with the "best" toy?

In your guidance, I'll try new cereals and, as years unroll, new thoughts, ideas, and concerns. Here's the cereal deal: If I buy it, they have to eat it—down to the last flake. Then they can have the toy.

When it comes to making choices, there's no better teacher than disappointment. And where is it safer than served in a cereal bowl? There's no better lesson than having to eat your words: I gotta have it!

Help me teach discernment in these early years; gullibility is more bitter to swallow in the big choices that come later.

Bad Words

I have calmed
    and quieted myself
    like a weaned child on its mother;
I'm like the weaned child on me.

—PSALM 131:2

"MOMMY, WHAT DOES THAT MEAN?"

Dear God, I feel faint! My sweet child is being contaminated by outside influences.

Move me past my first reaction—to wash mouths out with soap. Guide me to let the kids approach me about, and with, anything—even bad words.

Inspire me as I explain why such talk isn't OK to use, but sharing it with me is. Calmness today is an investment: by the time teen years arrive, taking words, ideas, lyrics, and concerns to Mom will be a habit.

Keep me shockproof.

Careless with My Words

Let us then pursue
what makes for peace
and for mutual upbuilding.
—ROMANS 14:19 NRSV

DEAR GOD, I tremble at my power: what I do is imitated; what I say, believed. Keep reminding me that a child raised with dire predictions will spend life butting against them like a firefly in a jar.

Forgive me when I'm careless with my words: "If you don't do _____, no one will like you. You're bad ... slow ... not like your sibling ... more trouble than you're worth."

How your heart must break when I proclaim life-limiting beliefs. Thumper, the bunny in Bambi, was taught well by his mama: "If you can't say something nice, don't say nothin' at all"—your wisdom in a fable. Help me heed it.

A Mother's Apology

"I am making all things new."
—Revelation 21:5 NRSV

THE APOLOGY STICKS CROSSWAYS in my throat like a fishbone.

God of second chances, I blew it with the kids big time. I could explain, justify, defend—or lie or keep quiet. If I confess and apologize, what will they think of me?

The truth is, dear God, that I am just your taller, older child; that I fail; that I am sorry. Give me the courage to say so.

I am grateful for your reassuring reminder that I don't need to be perfect, just honest. Be with me as I pass on this wisdom and your graceful promise: "I am making all things new"—even today's blunder.

"Why, Mommy?"

"Ask.... Search.... Knock."

—MATTHEW 7:7-8

KIDS ASK the darndest questions: Why do bad people win? Why do pets, friends, family members die too soon? Why do friends turn against me?

I wonder, too, eternal God.

Mothers are supposed to have answers; help me live with my ignorance. Give my children patience as I scramble for explanations to their insatiable quest to learn why. Remind me that I don't need all the answers, just a willingness to consider the questions and honor the questioners.

Knock, seek, ask—imperative verbs implying your blessing on our quests.

No More Patience

I will try to walk a blameless path,
but how I need your help, especially in my own home,
where I long to act as I should.

—PSALM 101:2 TLB

GOD, TODAY MY PATIENCE is as thin as onion skin. I've had it with the kids. I put on an armor of righteous indignation. *Come, valiant God, join me in battle with these upstart, annoying kids.*

In the mirror, I appear strong, formidable—tight jaw, steely eyes. I rehearse: *I am the mother, and this is my house.* Ultimatums roll from my mouth. And then I feel your restraining hand.

Bridges, not walls, you say. *Find another way. Negotiate; don't annihilate.*

I'll try, I mumble, *beginning with myself.* Practicing what I preach, I give myself a time-out, for I feel cranky and mean—not fit company to work things out. Thank you, God, for intervening.

A Rough Day

Even when I walk
through the darkest valley,
I fear no danger
because you are with me.

—PSALM 23:4

IT HAS BEEN A ROUGH DAY. First the car battery died, then I nearly stepped on a snake, and now this!

Give me a minute, God. I need to collect myself in the wake of this last catastrophe at the hands of my child.

Help me remember that I have a choice. Which response will lead me closer to the mom I want to be?

Remind me that you promised to accompany me through the valleys. Give me energy to make the trek and bring the kids along; today is not a great place to get stuck.

My Efforts Seem Useless

Now faith, hope, and love remain—these three things—and the greatest of these is love.

—1 Corinthians 13:13

SOMETIMES MY MOTHERING efforts seem as useless as dust in the wind. Will anything I do last?

God of promise, send me doves as you sent the Noah family, so I will know that at least I'm heading in the right direction.

Tell me, O God, what lasts.

Relationships of love, you remind me.

Love, steadfast and loyal, despite tantrums or errant choices. Love, patient and humorous. Love, offered without strings. Love, invested without requiring guaranteed return. Love, as I feel it from you, landing dove-soft on my outstretched hands, folding them into hugs around my children.

If Only

You are a God ready to forgive,
merciful and compassionate,
very patient, and truly faithful.

—NEHEMIAH 9:17

NOT A DAY ENDS, God of fresh starts, that I don't say, "If only I could do it over." I regret what I said or did—or didn't say or do. I cling to Nehemiah's assurance that "you are a forgiving God."

Keep me from getting stuck in the rut of shame; send me to apologize. Make me wise enough to learn from the mistakes that have something to teach me and to discard those that, like out-of-season clothes, are useless.

I wish our days could be rewound and played again, like old home movies. Since they can't, I will move from this moment, in your fortifying grace, knowing that I will do better.

Cleaning Out My Soul

"Who among you by worrying can add
a single moment to your life?"

—Matthew 6:27

LORD OF LASTING TREASURES, I am piling here, piling there, sorting stuff for a garage sale. Like my closets, my soul is overcrowded. What, I worry, do I need in order to be a good mother? Guide my sorting:

Keep humor; *toss* battles of will.

Keep tolerance and imagination; *toss* inflexibility and overreactive fear.

Keep respect and acceptance of my kids just as they are today; *toss* supermom lists and myths—ditto for others' expectations.

Guided by you, my sorting will continue as I toss out useless worrying habits—bell-bottoms of the soul.

Broken Pieces, Mended Hearts

We know that all things work together
for good for those who love God.

—ROMANS 8:28 NRSV

BOOM. The vase breaks into a million pieces. "Mama fix," the little one says.

Right. Mama fix—toys, wallpaper the baby pulled loose, a tree the mower nicked, schedule. Mama fix.

Yet, redeeming God, such certainty is how I approach you. I feel you inspiring me to glue vase shards to a pillar candle and brush it with melted wax for a centerpiece.

Things get broken, plans change. And in your grace, mothers are good at contingency plans. So are kids. They love nothing better than cutting, pasting, and gluing back together. With you, our disasters can yield treasures.

Single Mother

I have learned
how to be content
in any circumstance.
—PHILIPPIANS 4:11

GOD OF WHOLENESS, how many halves make a complete family? This is the new math of single parenting, and I'm dizzy from tallying up all the loose ends.

I often feel incomplete, for our family portrait looks as if something might be missing. Yet, O God, it's not missing much that matters. We have love—love for one another, love for and from you, love enough to include someone else if that happens.

Relieve me of defending or compensating. There's more than one way to add up what equals a good family—families are far more than the sum of their parts. Help me focus on what we do have.

Who's Mom's Favorite?

The sun has one kind of glory,
the moon has another kind of glory,
and the stars have another kind of glory.

—1 CORINTHIANS 15:41

MY KIDS SQUABBLE, God, about who's the favorite. Which child *is* my favorite? Do I love them equally?

Give me the wisdom of Solomon, so that truth can set us free—free from needless jealousy and anxiety.

Just as you tend your earthly children, loving Parent, guide me to love equally—yet not the same. When one child needs more, I will be *there*. Another time, when a different child emerges with the strongest need, I will be *there*.

Help my kids know that Mom's love is as limitless as the cosmos. In my sky, there's room for all my kids to be stars.

Outsmarting the "Monsters"

Why...
   are you so depressed?
   Why are you so upset inside?
Hope in God!

—PSALM 42:5

MONSTERS MAY NOT BE in the closet or beneath the bed, God of light, but they seem to be everywhere else. As mothers with vigilant eyes, we see it all: lost milk-carton children, baby snatchers, molesters, drunk drivers.

Help me rear my kids to be cautious, not fearful, by first dealing with my fear. Equip me to lead them through the valleys of enemies. Galvanize me into prevention and intervention so that I may help rebuild your world. Kids need doers, not worriers. Let hope be the last word in the bedtime stories I tell.

Cleaning Up Life's Playground

*Train children in the right way,
and when old, they will not stray.*

—Proverbs 22:6 NRSV

GOD OF PLAY, what is life's playground teaching our kids?

Forgive me for my cynicism, as toxic as any toy, video, or lyric. Help me trust the process of talking and choosing rather than forbidding and eliminating. Give me patience with the little ones to "show and tell" what's not OK. Fortify me to "check out" videos and lyrics with my teens. Give me bright eyes to spot creative "stuff" that will bring a sense of wonder and joy.

Keep me from being a wet blanket on life's playground, Lord, but let's clean it up a bit. It's not fit for children— of any age.

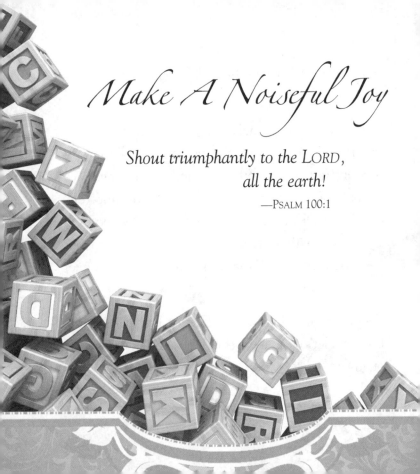

Make A Noiseful Joy

Shout triumphantly to the LORD,
all the earth!

—Psalm 100:1

BLOCKS TUMBLING, toy trucks revving, dollies chattering, children squealing. I have a colossal headache. Thank you, God, for shushing me before I could yell, "Stop this noise!"

Noise? It's a symphony of love, play, and discovery. At your inspiration, I am adding to it, offering pie-plate tambourines and dishpan drums. Is there a better place to live than in a band of children so pleased with their place in creation that they can't help dancing and shouting?

Help me listen between the beats of my headache to hear hearts overflowing with joy. Join our parade, God of music and motion—it's in your honor. Let us all make a "noiseful joy."

Lighten Me Up, Lord

He will still fill your mouth with joy,
your lips with a victorious shout.

—Job 8:21

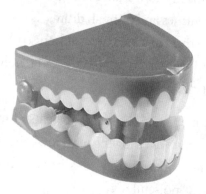

IT'S BETTER TO LAUGH than cry over spilled milk, for it happens a lot with kids.

Bloopers, blunders, spills, and splatters are putting permanent lines on my face. Which shall I choose, laughs or frowns?

Erase these faint frowns that are forming; forgive my tight-lipped annoyance. Lighten me up, Lord, from the dark sourpuss who needs to laugh at herself so that she can laugh with the kids.

Thank you for the gift of laughter. It's one that kids understand—giggles are on infant lips before words. Chuckle along with me at my next blunder, God, so that with your help, I'll be first to laugh.

My Adopted Child

I prayed for this boy, and the LORD gave me
what I asked from him.

—1 SAMUEL 1:27

This is what I have asked
of God for you:
that you will be… knit together
by strong ties of love.

—COLOSSIANS 2:2 TLB

AS MYSTERIOUSLY as if I'd fashioned sunflowers from air, a new person now lives where once there was none. A child, dear God—my adopted child.

I am forever changed.

There is a wondrous greening of my soul. No longer a woman only, I am now also a mother. Ah, but this child and I are more than a splitting of cells in the tapestry of a womb; we are chambers in each other's hearts.

Family Traditions

LORD, through all the generations
you have been our home!
—PSALM 90:1 TLB

DO SOMETHING ONCE with a child and it becomes tradition—where to hang the holiday star, what to eat on a picnic, which path to take.

Dear God, make our family traditions worthy, for like knots on a string, they lead us forward and backward. I name my childhood traditions to you in thanksgiving: _____

What transforms ordinary events into lifelong traditions? What makes paper chains into holy relics and gluey, lopsided homemade gifts into icons?

Love.

Inspire me to show my kids the divine love, the holiness, in the ordinary.

Mother of a Teen

Let love guide your life.
—COLOSSIANS 3:14A TLB

DEAR GOD, can you hear me above the stereo? Once the music is cranked up and the clothes become weird, you know you're the mother of a teen. God, help me; I'm there.

Help me understand that this child is more fragile than an unborn babe, for now my shelter has been outgrown. Bless this unattractive but essential stage; like a butterfly, this new creature must beat against its cocoon to become strong enough to fly. One day this child will soar to unimaginable heights. Focus me on that, instead of the junk on the floor, the strange clothing, and what passes as music. And by the way, thanks for the inspiration to buy stereo earphones.

Peer Pressure

Even children make themselves known by their acts.

—Proverbs 20:11 NRSV

HOW YOUNG ARE THEY, O Lord, when they first whine, "But everybody's doing it." I was outnumbered when my child spotted another child. Peer pressure was born in that instant. Are you and I, gentle Leader, really outnumbered?

Help me lure them toward independence, not sheeplike conformity. Help me respect their need to belong to their world; help me find a way to link it to mine. For that, resourceful God, send me peers who support mutual standards.

Then, when the kids protest, I can say with a smile, "But everybody's doing it."

If you can't beat 'em, join 'em.

Helping Teens Choose Wisely

Teach a child to choose the right path.
—Proverbs 22:6 TLB

MY CHOCOLATE CRAVING is no temptation at all compared to those temptations facing my teens. They're bombarded by hormones and media, and peers flaunting freedoms they don't have; they're ridiculed for being smart, clean, sober.

Keep me approachable, Lord. Inspire me with "cool" ways to help them see beyond the next party, toke, drag, or drink. Help me bolster and applaud their ability to choose wisely. Keep me calm and reassuring, for although they dare not admit it, their world scares them, too. Make me worthy of setting a standard by offering options, and make me strong enough to maintain it.

Mom's Law

No discipline is fun while it lasts,
but it seems painful at the time.
Later, however, it yields the peaceful
fruit of righteousness for those
who have been trained by it.
So strengthen your drooping
hands and weak knees.

—HEBREWS 12:11-12

INSPIRED BY YOU, God, I'm giving my kids excuses to be different with a simple phrase: "My mom won't let me—she's the meanest mom in the world." It's a great protector against peer insistence.

Give me broad shoulders to carry the weight of this title. When I stumble, keep me steadfast. Kids need the security of boundaries and consequences. At the same time, help me know when I should flex or toss outgrown rules. Help me mix freedom with obedience, the loving formula you use with me.

My Teen and I Need You, God

Let us then pursue what makes for peace
and for mutual upbuilding.

—ROMANS 14:19 NRSV

LIKE TWO HALVES of a walnut, my teen and I need you, God. We're both shrill; we both threaten to disown, run. At your knee, God of all generations, we pray:

Hear the cries of mothers baffled by adolescent children. Hear the pleas of these children who yearn to be free yet are afraid and angry at their own fear. Hear the pleas of both, who need dialogue, even as they appear to reject it.

Give us wisdom to learn from each other, inviting debate, welcoming new ideas. Lead us to common ground and help us find peace within—so that neither mother nor child needs to run away from home. Amen.

Holding My Tongue

Don't scold your children so much that they
become discouraged and quit trying.

—Colossians 3:21 TLB

SIT ME DOWN and close my mouth, O God. I poke too deeply into the kids' lives. But it feels good to be needed. And, in my defense, I'm usually correct.

Forgive my arrogance, for being correct doesn't matter: The effect is crippling.

The kids flounder in needless confusion.

Help me show support, not imply doubt. Teach me how to back off, chill out, get a grip, get a clue, get a life of my own.

May I be resource and companion, not a know-it-all busybody. Guide me to assure my kids, as you do, with, "I am with you always" (Matthew 28:20 TLB), then ease into the background. They'll know where to find me.

Picture Me, a Stepmother!

If anyone is in Christ, that person is part of the new creation. The old things have gone away, and look,

new things have arrived!
All of these new things
are from God, who
reconciled us to himself
through Christ and who
gave us the ministry of
reconciliation.

—2 CORINTHIANS 5:17-18

SOMEONE ELSE'S CHILD, O God, stares at me across the table, wary, watching—my stepchild. I'm grateful for this fledgling family. It's good to celebrate renewal—however it is found.

Heal old wounds. Help me put kids' needs before mine, blending old and new in delicate touches, like the watercolor painting on the refrigerator. I peer closely at it—our new family portrait. Yep, there you are, Lord, smack dab in the heart of our family bosom.

Accepting My Teen

Everything that has been created by
God is good, and nothing that is
received with thanksgiving
should be rejected.

—1 Timothy 4:4

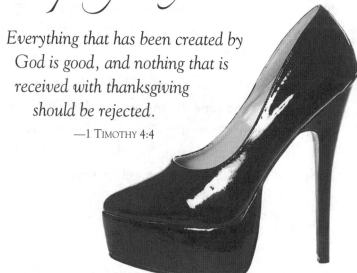

I'D LIKE TO SEND this note to school with my teen: "My mother didn't dress me." I confess I want to create my child in an image that will flatter me—and it's not just about clothes.

Guide me, God of acceptance, as I ponder how another's appearance really reflects upon me. Forgive my self-absorption.

God, do you want to send a note with me: "I didn't intend her to be like this"? I'm grateful that you love me as I am, without disclaimers. Surely, I can too.

But dear God, can you believe the outfit that kid is wearing?

Fortify me for supporting the right to look foolish.

Minding My Manners

Those who trouble their family will inherit the wind.
—Proverbs 11:29

Each person should test their own work.
—Galatians 6:4

RUDE. DISRESPECTFUL. EMBARRASSING.

On my knees, I confess, merciful God, that this doesn't describe the kids; it's me. I humiliate my children with shrill, public scoldings. I yell; I speak sarcastically, rudely; I interrupt and shame them.

Tune me in to strident voices coming from the sandbox or from teens on phones or in school halls. My God, they echo me.

When scolding is needed, help me find a private spot, look eye-to-eye, and softly explain. In-your-face berating is intolerable; you never do it to me.

Mother's Intuition

We live by faith and not by sight.
—2 CORINTHIANS 5:7

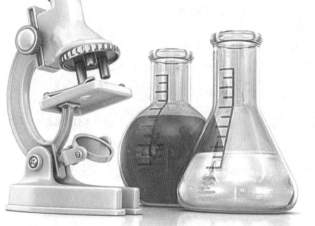

NO SCIENTIFIC TEST can confirm this bump of mother's intuition that allows me to know without evidence—a gift to last a lifetime and span any distance.

Knowing that you created me "wonderfully complex" (Psalm 139:14 TLB), I trust my gut—something is going on with my child.

Remind me, gentle Teacher, that not all insights require immediate action. Like Mary, some of what I know, I'd be wisest just to ponder—attuned, silent, ready to act. I trust that you will let me know when and where.

A Child's Poor Choices and a Mother's Broken Heart

I am convinced that nothing can ever separate us from [God's] love.

—ROMANS 8:38 TLB

FROM THEIR INFANCY, it's hard not to choose for our children. It's a riddle, O God, why you give us freedom to choose. Didn't you know it can break a mother's heart?

Comfort me as I cope with a choice not mine; forgive any role I had in it.

Keep me from saying, "I told you so."

Help me separate doer from deed; give me courage not to accept another's consequences. Can I be that strong? In your grace, I can, passing on your words to me: "Nothing can separate us"—not even poor choices.

Building Bridges, Not Walls

Unless it is the LORD who builds the house,
the builders' work is pointless.
—PSALM 127:1

SIT WITH ME, God of broken dreams, in the debris of my family.

Toddler tantrums, teen rebellion, young-adult resistance—it topples me as a tornado overturns a town. I'm tempted to finish the destruction with harsh words, yet how can I reject or give up on a child loved by you, no matter how great the upheaval?

Give me eyes like the green sunfish, which can see even in dark murky depths, so that I can salvage what's left in my darkness. Give me other reconstruction tools, too, for with you as Cornerstone, I'm building bridges—day after day.

Rubber-Band Resiliency

Those who hope in the LORD
will renew their strength.
—ISAIAH 40:31

YOU NAME IT, Lord, and I've seen it: chicken pox at Christmas; half the soccer team dropping in for supper; stray critters and kids on the doorstep—even, God forbid, big troubles. Thank you for the gift of resiliency.

I follow in the footsteps of eons of valiant women who raised kids while changing history. They bequeathed to me a fresh eye to see new responses, the courage to carry them out, and rubber-band resiliency. It lets me s-t-r-e-t-c-h, not break, in the pressure of daily life and the surprises that kids bring home—like stray puppies.

Keep me flexible.

Worrying About Tomorrow

Don't be anxious about tomorrow.
God will take care of your tomorrow too.
Live one day at a time.

—MATTHEW 6:34 TLB

IF I COULD see around the corner to the future, would I really want to? I'd probably just act more frenzied than I do now: organizing, preparing, trying to control, fretting.

Help me, God of tomorrow. Keep me busy as a pathfinder, showing my kids "how to" rather than "what" to live.

Inspire me to follow in the footsteps of ancient desert nomads who wore tiny lanterns on their shoes, to give enough light just for the next step. That's all I really need.

Remembering My Past

LORD, you have been our help,
generation after generation.

—PSALM 90:1

GOD OF THEN and now, there's nothing like a stroll down memory lane to put my teens into perspective. I'm grateful that you nudged me to look over my shoulder at my past.

My kids are poring over old yearbooks, souvenirs, and photos that measure me like growth rings on a tree. (*Don't you love their expressions?*) It's as difficult for them to imagine that their mom had a past as it is for them to imagine that their "now" is not forever.

Give me a ready laugh and an understanding heart; I've been there, done that. Give me wisdom to enable my kids to do likewise.

Thank You for My Mother

LORD, you have been our help,
generation after generation.

—PSALM 90:1

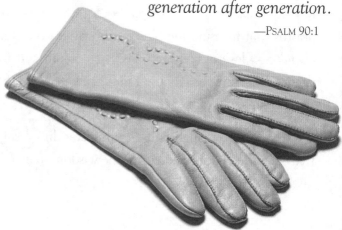

I WOKE THIS MORNING wearing my mother's hands like soft, worn gloves. In your continual re-creation, I also hear her voice in mine as I tend my children. I see her smile behind mine in the mirror. I make her recipes and pass on her truth-filled sayings, such as _____ to this newest generation, her heirs.

Thank you, loving God, for my mother. I kneel before her steadfast caring. I am a much-blessed daughter.

Sandwich Generation

He gives power to the tired and worn out,
and strength to the weak.

—Isaiah 40:29 TLB

A RIDDLE FOR YOU, wise God: Whom do I mother first, my aging parents or my children?

I'm pulled like a wishbone as I straddle generations, being mother to all: feeding, cleaning, chasing, lullabying. Keep me strong. Inspire solutions that include even the smallest kids helping out, for it takes a village to tend just about everyone.

And after they're all down for the night—bathed, diapered, and lullabied—hold me, the one in the middle, whose needs wait.

On the Sidelines

The Lord will protect you
on your journeys—
whether going or coming—
from now until forever from now.

—PSALM 121:8

WE KNOW this poem by heart, don't we, dear God? Join me in the audience as my child says it alone.

It's easier to say a poem—or kick the goal or rise on wobbly toes for a pirouette or go for a job interview—than to sit here sweating.

Help me get used to it, for this is where I belong. My presence on the sidelines is an assumption to be relied upon, just as yours is for me. Friends may be fickle, and fame may be fleeting, but Mom is always there—applauding like mad, with your hands over mine.

Thorny Nest

I am with you always,
  to the end of the age.
—MATTHEW 28:20B NRSV

GRADUATION LOOMS; college beckons. All that is left is dismantling a nest. I share my kids' ambivalence.

Dear God, give me the wisdom of Mother Eagle. With eaglets loaded on her wings, she flaps them off in the highest currents, catching them if they falter. Daily they venture and return to the nest—until she finishes untufting it of grasses and milkweed silks, leaving a framework of thistles and thorns.

With flying lessons nearly complete, I too feel I'm sitting on a thistle, even as I welcome my new independence. Steady me as I leave a few soft strands to assure those who must fly on, "You're never too far from home."

Letting Go

*Renew the thinking in your mind by the Spirit
and clothe yourself with the new person.*

—EPHESIANS 4:23-24

A MOTHER RELINQUISHING her grown-up child is a pitiful sight. My airy talk, dear God, of providing a child with "wings" is hollow, for I am tossing apron strings like a lasso around this one who is taking flight.

Forgive my sudden frights, my lack of trust in my child, myself, and you. I'd forgotten that you go both ways at once—with a departing child and with a left-behind mom.

With that assurance, I'll repaint my child's now-vacated room—blue, I think, the color of space.

Long-Distance Mother

There's a season for everything
and a time for every matter
under the heavens.

—ECCLESIASTES 3:1

THERE THEY GO—stroller, trike, bike, car, jet, train, moving van.

There they go—out of my arms and into their world. Steady me, dear God, as I pause at its threshold. I dare follow only at a distance, lest they see me hovering, thinking they can't make it alone—or worse, that I can't.

Help me find ways to show that I know we both can make it.

Help me reinvent myself, a long-distance mother.

There's Still Room on My Lap

If they are sad, share their sorrow.

—ROMANS 12:15 TLB

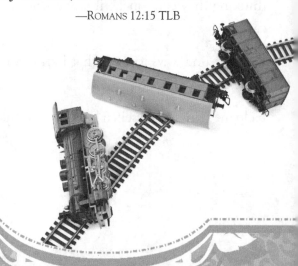

MY CHILD, now grown and gone, is back with a problem.

Help me, God who mends torn lives, as I gather this child close. Help me listen, not talk; stifle my temptation to say, "I told you so," or to fix it myself. As you do for me, I'll mirror back to this child the person you see. Be the resource that makes it possible.

Mothering was simpler when kids fit on my lap and problems could be fixed by kissing boo-boos and gluing broken toys. Thank you that I still have the knack. The boo-boos are just bigger.

Boomerang

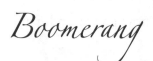

You have always cared for me...
now hear me as I call again.

—PSALM 4:1 TLB

LAUGH WITH ME, God of wanderers, at this greeting-card message: "The farther away they go, the harder they hit the wall when they return."

Adult kids are coming back to the nest. Gone is my hard-won freedom from listening, worrying, sharing the telephone, bathroom, and car. Gone is my new life.

Guide us to common ground; mediate our negotiations; inspire solutions and options. And for everyone's sake, dear God, help this be a brief stopover.

Where Did the Years Go?

Teach us to number our days
so we can have a wise heart.
—Psalm 90:12

WHERE DID the years go?

I willed the children to grow up.

Hurry, hurry, I prodded. Time couldn't go fast enough, I fretted. But, dear God, it did, taking childhood with it.

In your redeeming hands, I have mothering time again—not to go back but to go forward at a new, more enjoyable speed. Slow me down, so that I can spend these mothering days in time measured by the ticking of a grandmother's clock—one that knows how quickly toddlers become teens, become long-distance visitors, become parents themselves.

Finally, I've learned to tell time.

What Is a Good Mother?

You must love the Lord your God with all your heart,
with all your being, and with all your mind.
This is the first and greatest commandment.
And the second is like it:
You must love your neighbor
as you love yourself.

—Matthew 22:37-39

WISE GOD, what is a good mother? I ask experts and get checklists that give points for beds made and dishes washed. I flunk, for—God, help me—I'd rather build tent houses than tidy mine.

I ask a kid and hear, "She reads to me; makes my lunch; waits up for me; listens." I ask you and hear, "She loves God with all her heart, soul, and mind, and she loves others as she loves herself."

So that I can keep track, I need a "Growth Chart to Measure Mom." It will tell of kids embraced, not tolerated; kids invited, not overlooked; kids who laugh, venture, and know they are capable and connected to their God. Give me spunk to ignore anything that doesn't foster these things—anything that doesn't stem from love.

Also available from Abingdon Press

Scripture & Prayers

A Moment with God

FOR SUNDAY
SCHOOL TEACHERS

Scripture & Prayers

A Moment with God

FOR TEACHERS

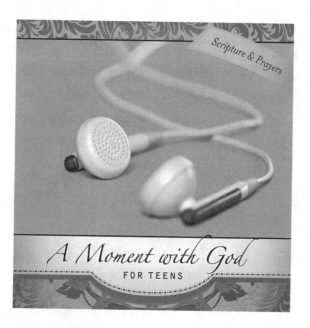

Scripture & Prayers

A Moment with God

FOR TEENS

Scripture & Prayers

A Moment with God

FOR THOSE
WHO GRIEVE

Scripture & Prayers

A Moment with God

FOR GRADUATES